Standardized Test
Preparation Workbook

Prentice Hall
Earth
Science

- Two Earth Science End-of-Course
  sample tests
- Additional practice tests reflect
  SAT II and ACT format

PEARSON

Prentice
Hall

Boston, Massachusetts
Upper Saddle River, New Jersey

ISBN 0-13-166254-6
6 7 8 9 10 10

CONTENTS

This workbook has been designed specifically to help you review science content you are learning this year and practice your science reasoning skills in preparation for standardized tests. In addition, it will help you prepare for national tests like the SAT II and the ACT. You will gain confidence in your test-taking skills as you work through the questions in this workbook.

Standardized Tests

This workbook enables you to practice taking tests that offer a mixed review of the earth science you learned during the year. There are 2 10-page practice tests that have been designed as end-of-course tests.

The multiple choice questions on the tests are designed to access different types of skills. Some questions require a straightforward recall of facts or concepts. Others require you to use your knowledge and understanding of earth science to interpret data, make inferences, or draw conclusions. Still others require that you know certain earth science concepts and be able to apply them to solve scientific problems.

SAT II and ACT Test Prep

The final section of the workbook provides the opportunity for you to become familiar with the question formats that are used on the SAT II and ACT.

NATIONAL SCIENCE EDUCATION STANDARDS CHART: TEST 1 AND TEST 2

National Science Education Standards

This chart identifies how each question in the Practice Tests correlates to the National Science Education Standards.

National Science Education Standards	Practice Test 1	Practice Test 2
Content Standard A: Science as Inquiry		
A-1: Abilities necessary to do scientific inquiry	1, 16	19
A-2: Understandings about scientific inquiry	7, 32	3
Content Standard B: Physical Science		
B-1: Structure of atoms	13	1, 20
B-2: Structure and properties of matter	15, 21, 36	28, 29
B-3: Chemical reactions	20	32
B-4: Motions and forces	22	17
B-5: Conservation of energy and increase in disorder	28	22
B-6: Interactions of energy and matter	29	33, 36
Content Standard C: Life Science		
C-1: The cell	5	25
C-2: Molecular basis of heredity	25	10
C-3: Biological evolution	12	5
C-4: Interdependence of organisms	33	2, 8
C-5: Matter, energy, and organization in living systems	6	11
C-6: Behavior of organisms	30	23
Content Standard D: Earth and Space Science		
D-1: Energy in the earth system	8, 35, 37, 38	14, 34
D-2: Geochemical cycles	4	7, 37
D-3: Origin and evolution of the earth system	9, 11	6, 35
D-4: Origin and evolution of the universe	31	16
Content Standard E: Science and Technology		
E-1: Abilities of technological design	17	27
E-2: Understandings about science and technology	23	4, 39
Content Standard F: Science in Personal and Social Perspectives		
F-1: Personal and community health	18	21
F-2: Population growth	3	15
F-3: Natural resources	10, 34, 39	9, 24
F-4: Environmental quality	26	12
F-5: Natural and human-induced hazards	14	31
F-6: Science and technology in local, national, and global challenges	27	30, 38
Content Standard G: History and Nature of Science		
G-1: Science as a human endeavor	19	18
G-2: Nature of scientific knowledge	24	13
G-3: Historical perspectives	2	26

© Pearson Education, Inc., publishing as Pearson Prentice Hall. All rights reserved.

Name _____ Date _____ Class _____

PRACTICE TEST 1

1. What is a scientific hypothesis?

   A an idea that is well tested and widely accepted by the scientific community

   B a clear list of observations from the natural world

   C a set of data for the given experiments

   D a possible explanation for why things happen in the manner observed

2. The Italian scientist Galileo is known for

   A being the first person to use a telescope for astronomical observations.

   B discovering the existence of the Earth's core.

   C inventing the system of calculus.

   D first identifying igneous rock.

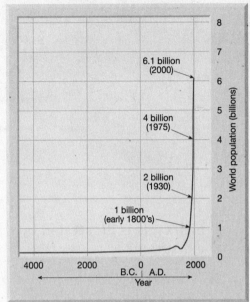

Growth of World Population

3. Which statement is supported by the population graph?

   A The population of the world has remained steady for the past two thousand years.

   B The world's population has increased dramatically over the past hundred years.

   C The world's population peaked in 2000 and is now in decline.

   D The world's population has always increased and has never decreased.

GO ON

Name _____ Date _____ Class _____

PRACTICE TEST 1 *(continued)*

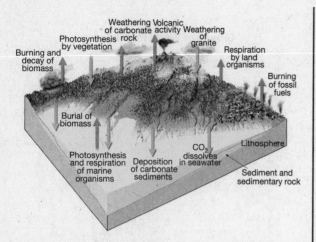

4. Which cycle is illustrated by the diagram?

   A water cycle

   B rock cycle

   C diamond cycle

   D carbon cycle

5. Which is not a primary marine producer?

   A crabs

   B bacteria

   C larger algae

   D phytoplankton

6. Coal, oil, and natural gas are all energy sources formed from

   A plant and animal material that has been transformed over millions of years.

   B nuclear decay of unstable radioactive substances.

   C hydrothermal energy that has been absorbed by underground rock.

   D materials ejected by the sun before life appeared on Earth.

7. Which statement does not support the idea that all the continents were once joined together?

   A Mesosaurus fossils are found in both South America and Africa.

   B Several mountain belts end on one coastline and reappear on the coastline of another continent.

   C There is no sign of a land bridge between Africa and South America.

   D Glacial deposits show that many continents may have once been in different positions than they are now.

GO ON

Earth Science Standardized Test Preparation Workbook: Practice Test 1 ▪ **2**

© Pearson Education, Inc., publishing as Pearson Prentice Hall. All rights reserved.

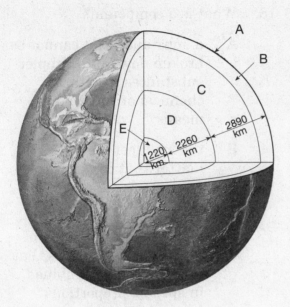

8. Which letters point to the upper and lower mantle?

   A   A and B

   B   B and C

   C   C and D

   D   D and E

9. The sun produces energy through nuclear fusion, converting

   A   hydrogen into helium.

   B   helium into hydrogen.

   C   oxygen into carbon.

   D   carbon into oxygen.

10. Where does the United States get nearly 90 percent of the energy it uses?

    A   solar power

    B   hydroelectric power

    C   atomic fuels

    D   fossil fuels

11. Which substance was not originally found in Earth's atmosphere?

    A   water vapor

    B   oxygen

    C   nitrogen

    D   carbon dioxide

12. During which era did plants that could survive on land first evolve?

    A   Cenozoic

    B   Precambrian

    C   Mesozoic

    D   Paleozoic

GO ON

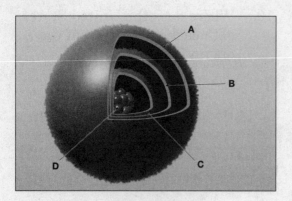

13. In the atom above, the structure at point D

   A   contains electrons and protons.

   B   contains neutrons and electrons.

   C   contains only electrons.

   D   has a positive charge.

14. Which is not a way to control erosion?

   A   construct windbreaks

   B   terrace hillsides

   C   remove vegetation

   D   plow along the contours of hills

15. What is a compound?

   A   a substance that cannot be broken down into simpler substances by either chemical or physical means

   B   the smallest particle of matter that contains the characteristics of an element

   C   a substance consisting of two or more elements that are chemically combined in specific proportions

   D   an atom with the same number of protons but a different number of neutrons

16. A friend asks you to help him identify a piece of rock. Which of the following strategies would probably not be helpful?

   A   breaking the rock to look at the inside

   B   examining the rock with a magnifying glass

   C   determining the temperature of the rock

   D   looking through a geology book to try to find a picture of the rock

GO ON

PRACTICE TEST 1 (*continued*)

17. What setup would best model how soil and water are heated differently? In each case, assume that you will measure the temperatures of both substances after ten minutes.

   A Place two beakers of water under different heat sources.

   B Place two beakers of soil under the same heat source.

   C Place a large beaker of soil and a small beaker of water beneath the same heat source.

   D Place two beakers with equal amounts of soil and water under the same heat source.

18. Which of the following is not one of the known health effects of water pollution?

   A nervous and reproductive system disorders

   B typhoid

   C birth defects

   D fish and other food sources become more nutritious

19. One of the best known discarded scientific hypotheses is

   A tectonic plate movement.

   B the Earth-centered model of the universe.

   C the water cycle.

   D transform fault boundary movement.

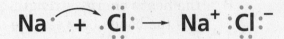

20. What does the diagram show?

   A sodium gaining an electron from chlorine

   B sodium and chlorine bonding without transfer of electrons

   C sodium giving up an electron to chlorine

   D sodium and chlorine sharing electrons and protons

GO ON

21. When heat is transferred to a glass of ice water, the temperature of the ice water remains a constant 0°C until all the ice has melted. The ice water's temperature does not rise because

   A   the heat's energy breaks apart the crystal structure of the ice cubes.

   B   the heat's energy strengthens the bonds between the ice molecules.

   C   the ice cubes give off latent heat, which slows down the melting process.

   D   evaporation and melting must occur simultaneously, otherwise no temperature change occurs.

22. Sir Isaac Newton was first to

   A   say the sun is the center of our solar system.

   B   argue that telescopes be used to study space.

   C   formulate and test the law of universal gravitation.

   D   discover inertia.

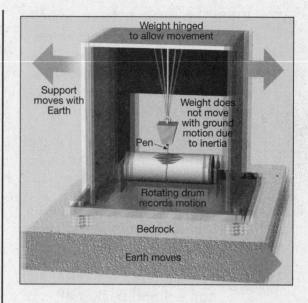

23. What would a scientist use the machine shown above to study?

   A   ocean waves

   B   the sun

   C   flora and fauna

   D   earthquakes

24. Which of the following is probably not a conclusion a geologist could draw using fossils?

   A   an area was once covered by water

   B   an area was once near a shoreline

   C   a certain rock layer is older than another

   D   an ancient earthquake had a magnitude of 4.6

>GO ON

25. DNA, a molecule found in the cells of every organism, determines an organism's traits. Over time, changes in DNA result in offspring that have different traits than their parents. Changes in DNA are fundamental to the evolution of species, and the progress of evolution can often be chronologically traced in the fossil record. Based on this information, which of the following is true?

    A   The DNA of organisms remains the same over time.

    B   Evolution and DNA changes are the same thing.

    C   Geologists look for DNA changes in certain rocks.

    D   DNA changes are key factors in evolution.

26. The ozone layer

    A   filters out UV rays.

    B   filters carbon monoxide.

    C   filters carbon dioxide.

    D   filters nitrogen.

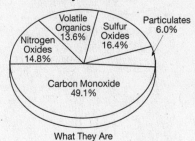

Primary Pollutants

What They Are

Where They Come From

27. Based on the diagram, which of the following is true?

    A   Transportation produces all of the carbon monoxide in the air.

    B   Nitrogen oxides make up most air pollution.

    C   Carbon dioxide makes up most air pollution.

    D   Transportation and industrial processes are the cause of most air pollution.

28. Which is not a method of energy transfer as heat?

    A   conduction

    B   carbonation

    C   radiation

    D   convection

> GO ON

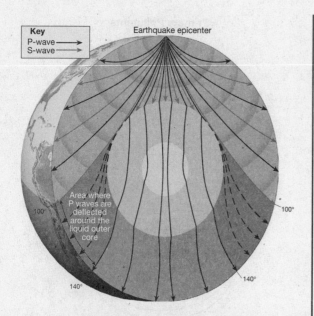

Key
P-wave ⟶
S-wave ⟶

Earthquake epicenter

Area where P waves are deflected around the liquid outer core

100°   100°

140°   140°

29. Which of the following is not true of the waves radiating from the earthquake's epicenter?

A They are seismic waves.

B They carry energy.

C They are strongest far from the epicenter.

D They are strongest closest to the epicenter.

30. Marine organisms are classified based on the following behaviors: where they live and how they move. All of the following are marine classifications except

A plankton.

B nekton.

C benthos.

D auroras.

31. According to the big bang theory, the universe began

A about 13.7 million years ago.

B about 13.7 billion years ago.

C about 13.7 trillion years ago.

D about 137,000 years ago.

32. Which of the following is not one of the reasons that the big bang theory is widely accepted?

A The universe appears to be expanding.

B Cosmic background radiation may be left over from the big bang.

C The sun is at the center of our solar system, not the Earth.

D Galaxies further away appear to be moving away faster than galaxies which are closer.

GO ON

PRACTICE TEST 1 (continued)

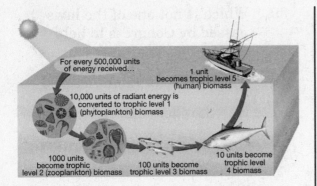

For every 500,000 units of energy received...

1 unit becomes trophic level 5 (human) biomass

10,000 units of radiant energy is converted to trophic level 1 (phytoplankton) biomass

1000 units become trophic level 2 (zooplankton) biomass

100 units become trophic level 3 biomass

10 units become trophic level 4 biomass

33. The diagram shows that

   A energy flows from trophic level 5 to trophic level 1.

   B energy is transferred efficiently between levels.

   C For every 500,000 units of energy put in, only 1 unit makes it to level 5.

   D The first step in the cycle is trophic level 3.

34. Which of the following is not a common source of groundwater pollution?

   A sewage from septic tanks

   B farm wastes

   C inadequate or broken sewers

   D carbon from igneous rock

35. The underlying cause of wind is

   A cold air from the polar ice caps.

   B geothermal energy released from the Earth's core.

   C sunspots.

   D the unequal heating of the Earth's surface.

36. A mineral's properties are determined by the elements that compose it and

   A its color.

   B how its elements are arranged.

   C whether the mineral was artificially or naturally created.

   D its streak test.

GO ON

PRACTICE TEST 1 *(continued)*

37. Which of the following is not one of the laws governing radiation?

A   Objects that are good absorbers of radiation are good emitters as well.

B   All objects, of any temperature, emit radiant energy.

C   In order for radiant heat to be transferred, either conduction or convection must take place.

D   Hotter objects radiate more total energy per unit area than colder objects do.

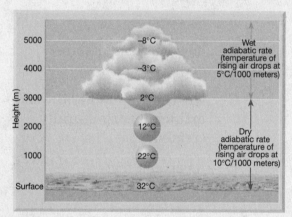

38. What happens at the 3000 meter mark in the diagram?

A   The latent heat increases.

B   The rising air cools to its dew point.

C   The rising air becomes compressed.

D   The water vapor in the rising air evaporates.

39. Which is not one of the laws passed by Congress to help protect our natural resources?

A   the Clean Land Act

B   the Clean Air Act

C   the Safe Drinking Water Act

D   the Clean Water Act

STOP

PRACTICE TEST 2

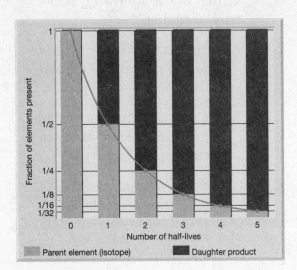

1. If 1/16 of the parent material remains in a sample, how many half-lives have passed?

    A   2

    B   3

    C   4

    D   5

2. Most ocean organisms get their food directly or indirectly from

    A   nekton.

    B   algae.

    C   benthos.

    D   hydrothermal vents.

3. Which of the following has not been a recent scientific discovery about Mars?

    A   The rover Opportunity found evidence of evaporite minerals associated with liquid water.

    B   Viking images have revealed ancient islands in what is now a dry streambed.

    C   Images from the Mars Global Surveyor indicate that groundwater has recently migrated to the surface.

    D   Discovery images have shown trace fossil remains of prehistoric bacterial life forms.

4. The science of oceanography

    A   draws on the methods of geology, chemistry, physics, and biology.

    B   concerns only the ocean's waters, not the ocean's floor.

    C   has been hurt by the overuse of sonar.

    D   has been hurt by the overuse of satellite imaging.

GO ON

5.   In the Cenozoic Era

A   mammals became the dominant land animals.

B   reptiles became the dominant land animals.

C   amphibians became the dominant land animals.

D   plants moved inland.

6.   According to the nebular theory

A   nebulas are composed of 92 percent helium and 7 percent hydrogen.

B   the solar system formed from a rotating cloud of dust and gas.

C   the solar system formed when two large asteroids collided.

D   the terrestrial planets produced the Jovian planets.

7.   Which of the following is not true of carbon?

A   In the atmosphere, it is found mainly as carbon dioxide.

B   Coal, oil, and natural gas are compounds made of carbon and hydrogen.

C   Some marine animals use it to produce calcite.

D   Pure carbon is very commonly found in nature.

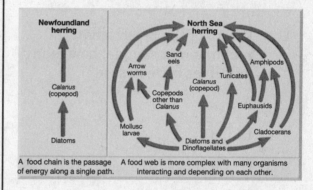

8.   Which of the following is true, according to the diagram?

A   Sand eels depend on the North Sea herring.

B   Diatoms depend on the Newfoundland herring.

C   The North Sea herring only has one source of food.

D   The North Sea herring can feed on amphipods.

GO ON

PRACTICE TEST 2 *(continued)*

9. Which is not a renewable resource?

   A   forest products

   B   plants for food

   C   natural fibers for clothes

   D   natural gas

10. When an organism reproduces, a molecule called DNA specifies the characteristics of the new organism. Occasionally, the DNA molecule changes, or undergoes a mutation. Some of these changes over time are evident in the fossil record. Based on this information, which of the following is true?

   A   Only advanced organisms contain DNA.

   B   Mutations in DNA might result in changes in an offspring's characteristics.

   C   DNA is not found in fossils, only living things.

   D   DNA was discovered by examining fossils.

11. Where do plants get carbon dioxide for photosynthesis?

   A   their cells

   B   water molecules

   C   the sun

   D   the air

12. Environmental science focuses on

   A   relationships between organisms and their natural environment.

   B   the movement of the heavenly bodies.

   C   the structure of rocks.

   D   the structure of atoms.

13. A geologist finds a fossil in a rock. The fossil seems to be the remains of an organism that scientists believe lived about 440 million years ago. The best hypothesis for the scientist to make is that

   A   the rock is much less than 440 million years old.

   B   the rock is much more than 440 million years old.

   C   the rock is around 440 million years old.

   D   there is no way to form a hypothesis from this information.

GO ON

PRACTICE TEST 2 *(continued)*

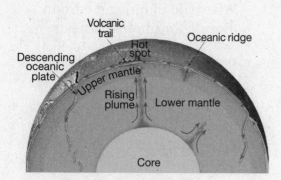

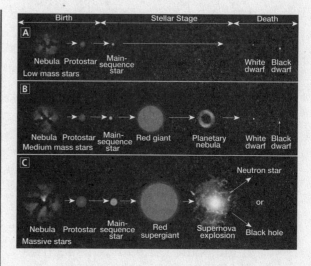

14. The diagram shows

    A   a hot spot.

    B   mantle convection.

    C   a batholith forming.

    D   a strike-slip fault.

15. One consequence of population growth is

    A   more renewable resources are available.

    B   the demand for resources increases.

    C   more nonrenewable resources are available.

    D   renewable and nonrenewable resources are more available.

16. Which of the following is true?

    A   All stars have a white dwarf phase.

    B   A low mass star forms a planetary nebula.

    C   Black holes are formed from medium mass stars.

    D   A massive star ends its life as a neutron star or a black hole.

17. Tides are produced by

    A   gravity only.

    B   inertia only.

    C   the outer planets.

    D   gravity and inertia.

GO ON

PRACTICE TEST 2 *(continued)*

18. To explain signs of ice sheets and alpine glaciers on areas too warm for them, some scientists suggested that glacial deposits had swept across the landscape in a catastrophic flood. Scientific evidence gathered during the nineteenth century showed

   A   this was absolutely correct.

   B   there was an extensive ice age that caused the glaciers and alpine ice sheets to move across the land.

   C   what scientists thought was caused by glacier movement was actually caused by erosion.

   D   what scientists thought was caused by glacier movement was actually caused by massive earthquakes.

19. If a hypothesis can't be tested

   A   it must be accepted.

   B   it is not scientifically useful.

   C   it is called a natural hypothesis.

   D   it is called an artificial hypothesis.

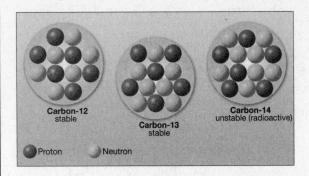

20. Each of the carbon isotopes

   A   has six neutrons.

   B   has six protons.

   C   is radioactive.

   D   has the same number of protons and neutrons added together.

21. Which of the following can be caused by an earthquake?

   A   landslides

   B   fires

   C   tsunamis

   D   all of the above

GO ON

22. What is the scientific definition of heat?

    A   a measure of the average kinetic energy of the atoms or molecules in a substance

    B   energy transferred from one object to another because of a temperature difference

    C   a measure of the bonds between atoms in a compound

    D   a sensation of warmth

23. Although the neritic zone only covers 5 percent of the oceans, many organisms choose to live there because

    A   photosynthesis occurs readily, nutrients wash in from the shore, and the bottom provides shelter.

    B   the intense darkness allows animals to protect themselves.

    C   high pressures make it easier for slow animals to escape predators.

    D   most species have adapted to the waves crashing on the beach.

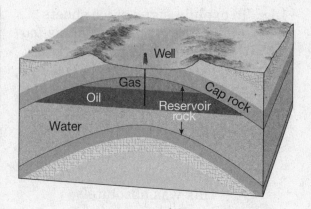

24. The oil did not evaporate from its reservoir because

    A   the cap rock sealed it in.

    B   oil does not evaporate.

    C   the water below it held it down.

    D   the gas held it down.

25. Energy from the sun is transformed into chemical energy in the oceans by

    A   producers.

    B   herbivores.

    C   carnivores.

    D   food webs.

GO ON

Name _____ Date _____ Class _____

PRACTICE TEST 2 *(continued)*

26. Johannes Kepler discovered

    A   how to make precise astro-
        nomical observations.

    B   Earth is a planet orbiting
        the sun.

    C   that matter can be
        converted to energy.

    D   three laws of planetary
        motion.

27. A model is a mental or physical
    representation of an object,
    process, or event. How might a
    model help a scientist or
    engineer plan a piece of
    technology?

    A   Before building an expen-
        sive robot, a smaller model
        is built. Based on the
        model, important changes
        are made before the real
        machine is created.

    B   An engineer builds a
        model building to discover
        how large of a shadow it
        will cast.

    C   Before a car is built, engi-
        neers construct a clay
        model to see how much
        wind resistance the car
        will have.

    D   All of the above are true.

28. How many atoms of oxygen are
    in the silicon-oxygen
    tetrahedron?

    A   one

    B   three

    C   four

    D   five

29. The atomic bonds of some
    minerals are weaker in certain
    places. These weak bonds are
    places where

    A   a mineral will break when
        stressed.

    B   a mineral is most pure.

    C   a mineral is most dense.

    D   a mineral is hardest.

GO ON

30. Which of the following is true of dams?

   A   They can help minimize flood damage.

   B   They can be used to create electric power.

   C   They can cause ecological damage to river environments.

   D   All of the above are true.

31. Why is the composite cone the most potentially dangerous type of volcano?

   A   They are built mainly of fluid basaltic lava flows.

   B   When they erupt, they eject a small amount of pyroclastic material.

   C   They generate the most explosive eruptions with the greatest amount of pyroclastic material.

   D   They erupt only once, so when they erupt they release a large amount of material.

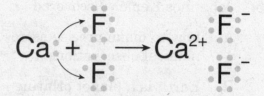

32. The diagram shows how fluorine and calcium atoms form the compound fluorite. According to the diagram, fluorite is

   A   a covalent compound.

   B   an ionic compound.

   C   a compound held together by metallic bonds.

   D   an elemental compound.

33. An electrical current is easily carried through

   A   covalent bonds.

   B   ionic bonds.

   C   metals.

   D   all of the above.

34. As latitude increases, the intensity of solar energy

   A   increases.

   B   decreases.

   C   stays the same.

   D   flashes.

GO ON

PRACTICE TEST 2 *(continued)*

35. About how long ago did oxygen begin to accumulate in Earth's atmosphere?

   A   2.5 million years ago

   B   25 million years ago

   C   2.5 billion years ago

   D   25 billion years ago

36. When an ocean wave moves through the water, the individual water particles move in a circle and

   A   the wave's energy moves in a circle as well.

   B   the wave's energy moves forward through the water.

   C   the wave's energy moves backward from the direction of the wave.

   D   the water particles far below the surface of the wave move in larger circles.

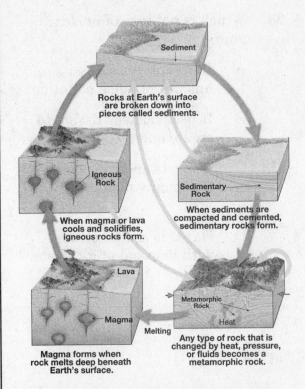

Rocks at Earth's surface are broken down into pieces called sediments.

Sediment

When sediments are compacted and cemented, sedimentary rocks form.

Sedimentary Rock

When magma or lava cools and solidifies, igneous rocks form.

Igneous Rock

Lava

Magma

Metamorphic Rock

Heat

Melting

Magma forms when rock melts deep beneath Earth's surface.

Any type of rock that is changed by heat, pressure, or fluids becomes a metamorphic rock.

37. What happens in the rock cycle after magma or lava cools to become igneous rock?

   A   It begins to be broken down at Earth's surface.

   B   It becomes a metamorphic rock.

   C   If it stays underground long enough it becomes sedimentary rock.

   D   Either A or B can occur.

GO ON

PRACTICE TEST 2 (continued)

38. Which is not true of nuclear energy?

   A   It creates an excessive amount of noise pollution.

   B   It uses nuclear fission to create energy.

   C   It meets about 7 percent of the energy demand of the U.S.

   D   Hazards are associated with disposal of its waste.

39. Which of the following is not an example of science being advanced by new technology?

   A   Modern technology allows us to send probes to distant planets to gather information.

   B   Using the telescope he had created, Galileo discovered that the planets were circular disks, not points of light.

   C   Radioactive dating allows geologists to date rock samples.

   D   Geologists can examine many layers of rock strata at the Grand Canyon.

STOP

SAT II PRACTICE TEST

Directions: *Each of the following questions or incomplete statements is followed by five suggested answers or completions. Select the one that is best in each case.*

1. The portion of Earth that includes the oceans is called the

   (A) atmosphere.
   (B) biosphere.
   (C) geosphere.
   (D) hydrosphere.
   (E) troposphere.

2. The smallest particle of matter that still contains the characteristics of an element is a(n)

   (A) atom.
   (B) compound.
   (C) electron.
   (D) neutron.
   (E) proton.

3. Atoms that lose or accept electrons form a(n)

   (A) atomic bond.
   (B) covalent bond.
   (C) hydrogen bond.
   (D) ionic bond.
   (E) metallic bond.

Questions 4, 5, and 6

   I. Igneous rocks
   II. Metamorphic rocks
   III. Sedimentary rocks

4. These rocks are classified by texture and composition.

   (A) I
   (B) II
   (C) III
   (D) I and II
   (E) II and III

5. These rocks are created through pressure.

   (A) I
   (B) II
   (C) III
   (D) I and II
   (E) II and III

6. These rocks are classified into granitic, andesitic, basaltic, and ultramafic.

   (A) I
   (B) II
   (C) III
   (D) I and II
   (E) II and III

SAT II PRACTICE TEST *(continued)*

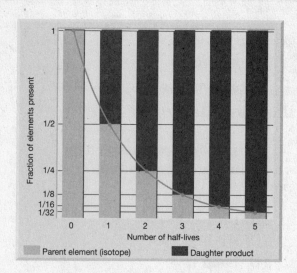

Parent element (isotope) ■ Daughter product

7. The information on the graph is used by geologists

   (A) to check the safety of radioactive materials.
   (B) to date fossils according to their rate of decay.
   (C) to estimate the formation and progress of metamorphism.
   (D) to calculate the amount of potential nuclear energy produced.
   (E) to analyze the content and origin of igneous rocks.

8. After three half-lives what percentage of daughter element exists?

   (A) 8%
   (B) 12.5%
   (C) 33%
   (D) 50%
   (E) 87.5%

9. A major force for chemical weathering is

   (A) frost wedging.
   (B) unloading.
   (C) water.
   (D) biological activity.
   (E) All of the above contribute to chemical weathering.

10. An oxbow lake forms from a(n)

    (A) meander.
    (B) floodplain.
    (C) levee.
    (D) delta.
    (E) tributary.

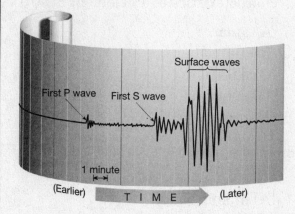

Questions 11 and 12

11. How much time passes between the start of the first P wave and the start of the first S wave?

    (A) 1 minute
    (B) 2 minutes
    (C) 3 minutes
    (D) 4 minutes
    (E) 5 minutes

GO ON ⟩

SAT II PRACTICE TEST *(continued)*

12. Which portion of the seismograph records activity that pushes and pulls?

    (A) The first P wave
    (B) The first S wave
    (C) The time difference between the waves
    (D) The surface waves
    (E) All of the measured waves

13. Which of the following best describes how Earth material moves in a slump?

    (A) A mass movement of material that falls freely through the air
    (B) A block of material moves suddenly along a flat, inclined surface
    (C) A block of material moves slowly along a curved surface
    (D) A mass movement of material that moves as a thick liquid
    (E) A mass movement that travels only a few millimeters per year

14. An area that has karst topography has largely been shaped due to

    (A) earthquakes.
    (B) volcanoes.
    (C) groundwater.
    (D) glaciers.
    (E) erosion.

15. Which of the following features is not created in front of a glacier?

    (A) Cirque
    (B) Lateral moraine
    (C) Ground moraine
    (D) End moraine
    (E) Kettle lake

16. Which of the following is a result of wind activity?

    (A) Loess
    (B) Sand dune
    (C) Desert pavement
    (D) Deflation
    (E) All of the above are caused by wind.

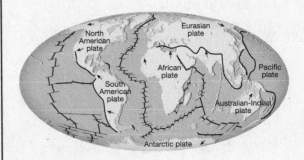

Questions 17 and 18

17. According to the map above, what type of plate interaction exists between South America and Africa?

    (A) They exist on the same plate.
    (B) They exist on plates that do not interact.
    (C) They exist on plates with a divergent boundary.
    (D) They exist on plates with a convergent boundary.
    (E) They exist on plates with a transform fault boundary.

GO ON

18. Which plate(s) previously made up Laurasia?

    (A) Eurasian
    (B) Australian-Indian and Eurasian
    (C) North American and Eurasian
    (D) African and Eurasian
    (E) African, Australian-Indian, and Eurasian

19. The most dangerous type of volcano is a

    (A) shield volcano.
    (B) cinder cone.
    (C) caldera.
    (D) composite cone.
    (E) lava plateau.

20. What type of geologic feature or activity is responsible for the creation of the Hawaiian islands?

    (A) A plume
    (B) A convergent plate boundary
    (C) A divergent plate boundary
    (D) A columnar rock
    (E) A batholith

Questions 21, 22, and 23
 I. Normal fault
 II. Reverse fault
 III. Thrust fault
 IV. Strike-slip fault

21. Which fault(s) is/are compressional in nature?

    (A) I
    (B) II
    (C) III
    (D) IV
    (E) II and III

22. Which fault(s) is/are horizontal in nature?

    (A) I
    (B) II
    (C) III
    (D) IV
    (E) II and III

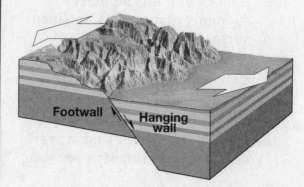

23. Which type of fault is shown above?

    (A) I
    (B) II
    (C) III
    (D) IV
    (E) This is not a fault.

GO ON

SAT II PRACTICE TEST *(continued)*

24. What usually occurs at an ocean-ocean convergence?

    (A) A continental volcanic arc forms
    (B) A volcanic mountain forms
    (C) An island arc forms
    (D) An accretionary wedge forms
    (E) A valley forms

25. Which of the following is indirect evidence of prehistoric life?

    (A) A mold
    (B) A cast
    (C) A trace fossil
    (D) A carbonization
    (E) A petrified fossil

26. Which of the following ages is the oldest?

    (A) Age of Reptiles
    (B) Age of Amphibians
    (C) Age of Fishes
    (D) Age of Invertebrates
    (E) Age of Mammals

27. Which of the following periods includes our present time?

    (A) Tertiary Period
    (B) Quaternary Period
    (C) Cretaceous Period
    (D) Permian Period
    (E) Pennsylvanian Period

28. The deepest parts of the ocean are made up of

    (A) deep-ocean trenches.
    (B) abyssal plains.
    (C) hydrothermal vents.
    (D) seamounts.
    (E) guyots.

29. The factors that affect seawater density are

    (A) temperature and depth.
    (B) depth and location.
    (C) biomass content and salinity.
    (D) salinity and temperature.
    (E) location and biomass content.

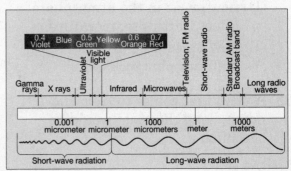

Questions 30 and 31

30. Which type of radiation has the longest wavelength?

    (A) Gamma rays
    (B) Visible light
    (C) Long radio waves
    (D) Microwaves
    (E) They all have identical wavelengths.

GO ON

SAT II PRACTICE TEST (continued)

31. Which type of radiation travels the fastest?

    (A) Gamma rays
    (B) Visible light
    (C) Long radio waves
    (D) Microwaves
    (E) They all travel the same speed.

32. The Coriolis effect describes

    (A) how the moon affects tidal patterns.
    (B) how Earth's rotation affects moving objects.
    (C) how temperature changes create pressure systems.
    (D) how gases in the atmosphere affect Earth's temperature.
    (E) how pressure and heat create metamorphic rocks.

33. A wind that comes in from the north along the coast would be classified as

    (A) cP.
    (B) cT.
    (C) mP.
    (D) mT.
    (E) mC.

34. Which of the following is a factor that increases the temperature of a climate?

    (A) The latitude of the location decreases.
    (B) The elevation of the location increases.
    (C) The location is downwind of a large body of water.
    (D) There is a large amount of vegetation in the location.
    (E) The location is on the windward side of a mountain.

35. Warm weather occurs during summer because

    (A) Earth is closest to the sun.
    (B) Earth is rotating at the slowest rate.
    (C) Earth has less precipitation and cloud cover.
    (D) Earth has a higher concentration of greenhouse gases.
    (E) Earth is tilted toward the sun.

GO ON

SAT II PRACTICE TEST (continued)

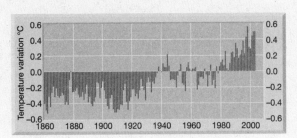

The figure above shows changes in Earth's average surface temperature.

36. According to the figure, which year had the highest average surface temperature on record?

    (A) 2003
    (B) 1998
    (C) 1985
    (D) 1909
    (E) 1863

37. What do scientists blame for the global warming trend?

    (A) A decrease in plant life
    (B) An increase in atmospheric gases
    (C) A change in Earth's rotational axis
    (D) An increase in acid rain
    (E) A decrease in the ozone layer

38. During a total eclipse of the moon,

    (A) Earth is completely in the penumbra.
    (B) Earth is completely in the umbra.
    (C) the moon is completely in the penumbra.
    (D) the moon is completely in the umbra.
    (E) Earth and moon are on opposite sides of the sun.

39. Which of the following planets does not fit easily into either the terrestrial or Jovian planet categories?

    (A) Earth
    (B) Uranus
    (C) Pluto
    (D) Mercury
    (E) Mars

40. Most of the sunlight emitted from the sun comes from the

    (A) photosphere.
    (B) corona.
    (C) chromosphere.
    (D) core.
    (E) prominence.

STOP

ACT PRACTICE TEST

Earth Science Test

DIRECTIONS: The passages below are each followed by several questions. After reading a passage, choose the best answer to each question. You may refer to the passages as often as necessary.

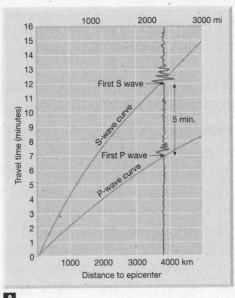

A

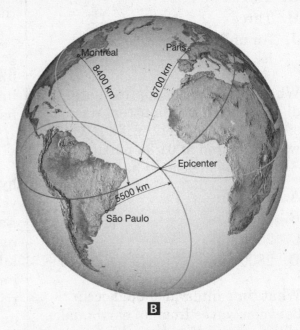

B

Passage I

A travel-time graph is used to determine the distance to the epicenter of an earthquake. The difference in arrival times of the first P wave and the first S wave in the graph is 5 minutes. So the epicenter is roughly 3800 kilometers away. The epicenter is located using the distance obtained from three seismic stations. The location in which the circles intersect is the epicenter.

1. According to the chart and illustration, what kind of data is needed to find an epicenter of an earthquake?

   A. Wave magnitudes of both P waves and S waves

   B. Distance between seismic wave occurrences

   C. Time between P wave and S wave occurrence

   D. Intersection of the P wave and S waves

ACT PRACTICE TEST *(continued)*

2. How many locations would be possible for an epicenter if only two seismic stations took measurements?

   F. One
   G. Two
   H. Three
   J. An unlimited number of locations

3. What would be the approximate distance from the Montreal seismic station to the epicenter if a P wave was measured at 01:36 pm and the S wave was measured at 01:40 pm?

   A. 1000 km
   B. 1500 km
   C. 2500 km
   D. 2800 km

4. What time interval should occur between waves from an earthquake with an epicenter that was approximately 1800 miles away?

   F. 2.5
   G. 3.0
   H. 4.0
   J. 4.5

Passage II

About 65 million years ago more than half of all plant and animal species died out in a mass extinction. This time marks the end of an era in which dinosaurs and other reptiles dominated the landscape.

The extinction of the dinosaurs is generally attributed to the group's inability to adapt to some radical change in the environment. What event could have caused the rapid extinction?

Hypothesis A

The most strongly supported hypothesis states that about 65 million years ago a large meteorite collided with Earth. The speed of the meteorite impact was believed to be 70,000 kilometers per hour. The force of the impact vaporized the meteorite and trillions of tons of Earth's crust. Huge quantities of dust and other debris were blasted high into the atmosphere. The encircling dust greatly restricted the sunlight reaching Earth's surface for months. Without sunlight for photosynthesis, delicate food chains collapsed. By the time the sunlight returned, more than half the species on Earth had become extinct.

There is some evidence to support the theory. A thin layer of sediment nearly 1 centimeter thick has been discovered worldwide. This sediment contains a high level of the element iridium, which is rare in Earth's crust but often found in meteorites.

GO ON

ACT PRACTICE TEST (continued)

Hypothesis B

Some scientists disagree with the impact hypothesis. These scientists suggest that huge volcanic eruptions led to the breakdown in the food chain. They cite enormous outpourings of lavas in northern India about 65 million years ago as support for their thesis. These scientists dispute the age of the crater in Mexico that meteorite theorists believe was the impact site. They believe that these volcanic eruptions released the iridium onto the surface and flooded the atmosphere with carbon dioxide, which caused the dramatic environmental changes.

5. According to Passage II, what event do the majority of scientists believe caused the dinosaurs to become extinct?

   A. A meteorite hit Earth, raising large levels of dust that blocked the sun and created conditions that made it difficult for plants to grow.

   B. A meteorite hit Earth, creating a large crater and scattering debris that made it difficult for most life forms to breathe.

   C. Large-scale volcanic eruptions and a catastrophic event such as a meteorite impact combined to create a break-down in the food chain.

   D. Increased levels of iridium from a meteorite impact or volcanic eruption caused disruptions in the environment that led to mass extinctions.

6. What kind of evidence do opposing scientists use to dispute the meteorite impact theory?

   F. They believe that iridium comes from volcanoes, not meteorites.

   G. They believe that the layer of iridium dust is not consistent world-wide.

   H. They believe that a meteorite could not have created enough damage to cause extinctions.

   J. They do not believe that the age of the impact crater is not consistent with the extinctions.

7. Which of the following statements is NOT a belief held by all scientists?

   A. A meteorite crashed into Earth 65 million years ago.

   B. A mass extinction took place 65 million years ago.

   C. A layer of iridium settled on Earth's surface 65 million years ago.

   D. Massive volcanic eruptions took place in India 65 million years ago.

8. Which piece of evidence is claimed as a part of both theories?

   F. Huge quantities of dust found in the atmosphere

   G. A layer of iridium in the rock layer

   H. Increased carbon dioxide levels in Earth's history

   J. A sudden decline in plant fossils

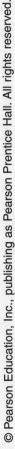

 GO ON

ACT PRACTICE TEST (continued)

9. What key element is indisputable for both teams of scientists in connection to the massive extinction?

A. Increased levels of carbon dioxide

B. An interruption in the food chain

C. A dramatic environmental change

D. Decreased levels of sunlight

10. What fact can you infer from the volcanic-activity theory?

F. Iridium is also found beneath Earth's crust.

G. Volcanic activity has caused other extinctions.

H. Photosynthesis is not dependent on carbon dioxide.

J. Dinosaurs were mostly plant-eaters.

Passage III

Relative humidity is a measurement used to describe water vapor in the air. In general, it expresses how close the air is to saturation. An investigation was conducted using a psychrometer to determine the relative humidity of air.

Part A. Calculating Relative Humidity from Water Vapor Content.

Relative humidity is the ratio of the air's water vapor content to its water vapor capacity at a given temperature. Relative humidity is expressed as a percent:

Relative humidity (%) = (Water vapor content/Water vapor capacity) × 100.

At 25°C, the water vapor capacity is 20 g/kg. The first part of the investigation involved taking data from three locations at 25°C and calculating the relative humidity.

Relative Humidity Determination Based on Water Vapor Content			
Air Temperature (°C)	Water Vapor Content (g/kg)	Water Vapor Capacity (g/kg)	Relative Humidity (%)
25	5	20	25
25	12		
25	18		

Part B. Determining Relative Humidity Using a Psychrometer.

A psychrometer consists of two thermometers. The wet-bulb thermometer has a cloth wick that is wet with water and spun for about 1 minute. Relative humidity is determined by the difference in temperature reading between the dry-bulb temperature and the wet-bulb temperature, and using Data Table 2. For example, suppose a dry-bulb temperature is measured as 20°C and a wet-bulb temperature is 14°C. The relative humidity would be 51 percent.

Data Table 2 Relative Humidity (percent)																					
Dry-bulb Tempera-ture (°C)	Depression of Wet-bulb Temperature (Dry-bulb Temperature − Wet-bulb Temperature = Depression of the Wet Bulb)																				
	1	2	3	4	5	6	7	8	9	10	11	12	13	14	15	16	17	18	19	20	21	22
−20	28																				
−18	40																				
−16	48	0																			
−14	55	11																			
−12	61	23																			
−10	66	33	0																		
−8	71	41	13																		
−6	73	48	20	0																	
−4	77	54	43	11																	
−2	79	58	37	20	1																
0	81	63	45	28	11																
2	83	67	51	36	20	6															
4	85	70	56	42	27	14															
6	86	72	59	46	35	22	10	0													
8	87	74	62	51	39	28	17	6													
10	88	76	65	54	43	33	24	13	4												
12	88	78	67	57	48	38	28	19	10	2											
14	89	79	69	60	50	41	33	25	16	8	1										
16	90	80	71	62	54	45	37	29	21	14	7	1									
18	91	81	72	64	56	48	40	33	26	19	12	6	0								
20	91	82	74	66	58	51	44	36	30	23	17	11	5	0							
22	92	83	75	68	60	53	46	40	33	27	21	15	10	4	0						
24	92	84	76	69	62	55	49	42	36	30	25	20	14	9	4	0					
26	92	85	77	70	64	57	51	45	39	34	28	23	18	13	9	5					
28	93	86	78	71	65	59	53	47	42	36	31	26	21	17	12	8	2				
30	93	86	79	72	66	61	55	49	44	39	34	29	25	20	16	12	8	4			
32	93	86	80	73	68	62	56	51	46	41	36	32	27	22	19	14	11	8	4		
34	93	86	81	74	69	63	58	52	48	43	38	34	30	26	22	18	14	11	8	5	
36	94	87	81	75	69	64	59	54	50	44	40	36	32	28	24	21	17	13	10	7	4
38	94	87	82	76	70	66	60	55	51	46	42	38	34	30	26	23	20	16	13	10	7	5
40	94	89	82	76	71	67	61	57	52	48	44	40	36	33	29	25	22	19	16	13	10	7

Relative Humidity Values

GO ON

ACT PRACTICE TEST *(continued)*

11. Follow the procedure in Passage III for calculating relative humidity using the water vapor content. What would you expect to fill in as the relative humidity when the air temperature is 25°C and the water vapor content is 18 g/kg?

    A. 25%
    B. 40%
    C. 60%
    D. 90%

12. What information must already be known before determining relative humidity based on the water vapor content?

    F. The water vapor content
    G. The water vapor temperature
    H. The water vapor capacity
    J. The water vapor depression

13. Which information is NOT needed to calculate relative humidity using the psychrometer?

    A. Dry bulb temperature
    B. Wet bulb temperature
    C. Water vapor
    D. Relative humidity values

14. Why were two temperature measurements needed to find the relative humidity in Part B of Passage III?

    F. To reduce the possibility of error
    G. To find an average
    H. To find a difference
    J. To create a range

15. Why is the relative humidity expressed as a percentage?

    A. The relative humidity is a measure of how much of the total volume of air is filled with water vapor.
    B. The relative humidity compares one temperature reading with another in terms of the percentage.
    C. The relative humidity is not an absolute measurement using any standard scale and is instead comparative.
    D. The relative humidity requires additional data to be used with the percentage in order to be applicable.

GO ON

Ocean Surface Currents

Passage IV

Huge, circular-moving current systems dominate the surfaces of the oceans. These large whirls of water within an ocean basin are called gyres. The ocean's circulation is organized into five major gyres, or circular current systems. The West Wind Drift flows around the continent of Antarctica. Use the map of Ocean Surface Currents to answer the questions below.

16. What type of currents make up the South Atlantic Gyre?

   F. Warm air currents
   G. Cold air currents
   H. Warm and cold air currents
   J. Warm and cold air drifts

17. What characteristic contrasts the gyres in the Northern Hemisphere with the gyres in the Southern hemisphere?

   A. Warm versus cold air currents
   B. Circular versus straight systems
   C. Clockwise versus counter clockwise rotation
   D. Equatorial versus non-equatorial currents

18. Which gyre does not include an equatorial current?

   F. The South Pacific Gyre
   G. The South Atlantic Gyre
   H. The Indian Ocean Gyre
   J. They all include an equatorial current.

GO ON

ACT PRACTICE TEST (continued)

19. Which current completely circles the Earth without interruption?

    A. The West Wind Drift
    B. The East Wind Drift
    C. The North Equatorial Current
    D. The South Equatorial Current

20. Which of the following continents is surrounded by either entirely warm-air currents or cold-air currents?

    F. North America
    G. Greenland
    H. South America
    J. Australia

Passage V

Communities are constantly looking for alternate ways to get the energy needed to serve their growing populations. When creating a power plant to supply a community without using fossil fuels, several options are available for consideration. Some of the most popular choices are between solar energy, nuclear energy, and hydroelectric power.

Solar Energy

Solar energy is the direct use of the sun's rays to supply heat or electricity. Solar energy has two advantages: the "fuel" is free, and it is non-polluting. Active solar collectors are used to heat water for domestic and commercial needs. For example, solar collectors provide hot water for more than 80 percent of Israel's homes. A solar collection facility heats water in pressurized panels. The superheated water is then transferred to turbines, which turn electrical generators.

There are a few drawbacks to solar energy. While the energy collected is free, the necessary equipment and installation is not. A supplemental heating unit is also needed when there is less solar energy, such as on cloudy days or in the winter. Solar energy is economical in some areas of the United States and will become even more cost effective as the prices of other fuels increase.

Nuclear Energy

Nuclear power meets about 7 percent of the energy demand of the United States. The fuel for nuclear plants comes from radioactive materials that release energy through nuclear fission. In a nuclear power plant the fission reaction is controlled by moving neutron-absorbing rods into or out of the nuclear reactor. The result is a controlled nuclear chain reaction that releases great amounts of heat. The energy drives steam turbines that turn electrical generators.

At one time, energy experts thought nuclear power would be the cheap, clean energy source that would replace fossil fuels. But several obstacles have slowed its development. First, the cost of building safe nuclear facilities has increased. Second, there are hazards associated with the disposal of nuclear wastes. Third, there is concern over the possibility of a serious accident that could cause radioactive materials to escape.

Hydroelectric Power

Hydroelectric power uses falling water to turn turbines and produce electricity. In the United States, hydroelectric

GO ON

ACT PRACTICE TEST (continued)

power plants produce about 5 percent of the country's electricity. Large dams are responsible for creating most of it by allowing a controlled flow of water.

Although water power is a renewable resource, hydroelectric dams have finite lifetimes. Rivers deposit sediment behind the dam, eventually filling the reservoir. This process takes 50 to 300 years and when it is filled, the dam can no longer produce power. The availability of suitable sites is an important limiting factor in the development of hydroelectric power plants. A good site must provide a significant height for the water to fall. Most of the best sites within the United States have already been developed.

21. What is the main advantage to using any of the three power-generating methods described instead of traditional fossil fuels?

   A. Each of the three methods described produce less pollution than traditional fossil fuels.

   B. Each of the three methods described provides more power than traditional fossil fuels.

   C. Each of the three methods described is safer than traditional fossil fuels.

   D. Each of the three methods described is more abundant than traditional fossil fuels.

22. Those that favor the use of nuclear power argue that its advantage over other alternative energy resources is based upon

   F. the quantity of energy obtained.

   G. the ease of setting up facilities.

   H. the availability of the resources needed to generate it.

   J. the absence of excessive waste products.

23. Which community described might be best suited to using solar power?

   A. A large coastal community in the Pacific Northwest.

   B. A small desert community in Nevada.

   C. A densely populated community inside of a large New England city.

   D. A moderately-sized community along the Mississippi River.

24. Which of the following is common to all three forms of alternative energy sources in generating large amounts of electricity for a community?

   F. All three sources involve generating some waste products.

   G. All three sources involve generating heat.

   H. All three sources involve turning turbines.

   J. All three sources are inadequate for supplying large amounts of power.

GO ON

ACT PRACTICE TEST *(continued)*

25. Which form of alternative energy is least sustainable over a long period of time?

   A. Solar energy

   B. Nuclear energy

   C. Hydroelectric energy

   D. All three forms are sustainable.

Passage VI

Most soils contain particles of different sizes. Soil texture refers to the proportions of different particle sizes. To classify soil texture, the U.S. Department of Agriculture has established categories based on the percentages of clay, silt, and sand in soil. The diagram shows how the percentages differ for each category. For example, point A represents a soil that is 40 percent clay, 10 percent silt, and 50 percent sand.

Texture strongly influences a soil's ability to support plant life. Sandy soils may drain quickly, while clay-rich soils drain very slowly. Plant roots often have difficulty penetrating soils that contain a high percentage of clay and silt. Loam soils are usually best for plant growth. They retain water better and store more nutrients than do soils composed mainly of clay or sand.

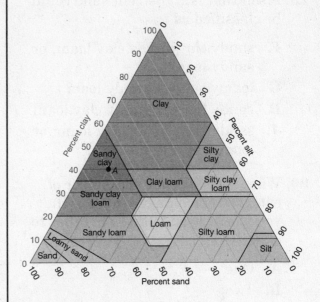

26. Which type of soil contains a higher percentage of silt?

   F. Silty loam

   G. Silty clay loam

   H. Loam

   J. Silty clay

27. What is the highest percentage of sand that can exist in a clay loam soil?

   A. 40%

   B. 43%

   C. 52%

   D. 80%

GO ON

ACT PRACTICE TEST *(continued)*

28. A soil that is 70 percent sand could be classified as

    F. sandy clay, sandy clay loam, or sandy loam.

    G. loamy sand or sandy loam.

    H. sandy loam or sandy clay loam.

    J. sandy clay, sandy clay loam, or loam.

29. What is the minimum number of category percentages in a soil that you would need to know in order to classify it?

    A. One

    B. Two

    C. Three

    D. None

30. Which type of soil would be best to use for gardening where rich soil with good drainage is important?

    F. Loamy sand

    G. Sandy loam

    H. Sandy clay loam

    J. Sandy clay

31. Which term describes a soil that is 60 percent silt, 30 percent clay, and 10 percent sand?

    A. Silty clay

    B. Sandy clay loam

    C. Silty loam

    D. Silty clay loam

Passage VII

Ocean water temperatures vary from equator to pole and change with depth. Temperature, like salinity, affects the density of seawater. However, the density of seawater is more sensitive to temperature fluctuations than salinity.

An experiment was set up to determine the effects of temperature on water density. The procedure is outlined below.

Part A

1. Mix cold tap water with ice cubes in a beaker. Stir until the water and ice are well mixed. Fill a graduated cylinder with 100 mL of cold water from the beaker. Make sure no ice gets into the graduated cylinder.

2. Put 2 to 3 drops of dye in a test tube and fill it half full of hot tap water. Pour the contents of the test tube into the graduated cylinder and record observations.

<u>Scientist's observation: The hot water stayed near the surface in the graduated cylinder.</u>

3. Add a test tube full of cold tap water to a beaker. Mix in 2 to 3 drops of dye and a handful of ice to the beaker. Stir the solution thoroughly. Fill the test tube half full of this solution. Do not allow any ice into the test tube.

4. Fill a second graduated cylinder with 100 mL of hot tap water.

5. Pour the test tube of cold liquid slowly into the cylinder of hot water. Record your observations.

>GO ON>

ACT PRACTICE TEST (continued)

Scientist's observation: The cold water sank beneath the warmer water in the graduated cylinder.

Part B

Idealized Ocean Surface Water Temperatures and Densities at Various Latitudes		
Latitude	Surface Temperature (C°)	Surface Density (g/cm³)
60°N	5	1.0258
40°	13	1.0259
20°	24	1.0237
0°	27	1.0238
20°	24	1.0241
40°	15	1.0261
60°	2	1.0272

32. Which information can you infer from the first observation made by the scientist?

F. The hot water was vaporized by contact with the colder water.

G. The hot water transferred some density through the dye to the cold water.

H. The hot water had a lower density than the cold water.

J. No information can be inferred from this one observation.

33. Which purpose does the dye serve in this experiment?

A. It acts as a control.
B. It acts as an identifier.
C. It acts as a measurement tool.
D. It acts as a timer.

34. Which statement best describes the relationship shown by the results?

F. Increased temperature causes an increase in density.

G. Increased temperature causes a decrease in density.

H. Increased density causes an increase in temperature.

J. Increased density causes a decrease in temperature.

35. How does the information from the first experiment apply to the information collected and presented in the table?

A. Warmer waters tend to collect at the top portions of the Earth.

B. Water near the warm-weather equator is less dense than other areas.

C. Warm water moves toward the ocean surface and is heated.

D. Water that moves in colder areas becomes less dense.

36. What could you imply about water location from this information?

F. Water in colder locations is less dense.

G. Water in colder locations is more dense.

H. Dense water moves to colder locations.

J. Dense water moves to warmer locations.

GO ON

ACT PRACTICE TEST (continued)

37. What information could you infer about ocean surface water temperatures and latitude?

- **A.** The degree of latitude has less of an effect than density.
- **B.** Density has more of an effect than the degree of latitude.
- **C.** The degree of latitude affects the temperature of surface water.
- **D.** Surface water has an increased temperature at increasing latitudes.

Passage VIII

Global warming is perhaps one of the most hotly debated environmental issues. Is the world getting warmer, and should society worry about it? Many scientists feel that global warming is an important issue that may have devastating consequences for the human race. Other scientists feel that the global warming issue is overblown and that there is very little need to worry. Below are two sides of the issue.

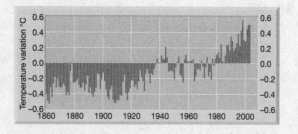

Opinion A

Global Warming is cause for alarm: As a result of increases in carbon dioxide levels, as well as other greenhouse gases, global temperatures have increased. The figure above shows that during the twentieth century, Earth's average surface temperature increased about 0.6°C. Scientists predict that by the year 2100, temperatures will increase by 1.4°C to 5.8°C. Warmer temperatures increase evaporation rates. This, in turn, increases the amount of water vapor in the atmosphere. Water vapor is an even more powerful absorber of radiation emitted by Earth than carbon dioxide. Therefore, more water vapor in the air will magnify the effect of carbon dioxide and other gases.

Temperature increases will also cause sea ice to melt. The melting of the ice will cause a substantial increase in the solar energy absorbed at the surface. This, in turn, will magnify the temperature increase created by higher levels of greenhouse gases. The melting of sea ice and ice sheets will also cause a global rise in sea level. This will lead to shoreline erosion and coastal flooding. Scientists also expect that weather patterns will change as a result of the projected global warming. Hurricanes will increase in number and intense heat waves and droughts will occur in some regions.

Opinion B

Global warming is not a threat: Some skeptics say the scientific models used to predict the climate do not deal with the planet's complex ecosystem. The atmosphere is too complex to be in a global model and then have integrated seasons years and centuries into the future. If it could be done, scientists say, then global modelers should be able to predict changes a year into the future, which they cannot do.

GO ON

ACT PRACTICE TEST *(continued)*

Although skeptics agree that the climate has changed recently, they believe that climate change is a natural phenomenon that does not pose a threat to humans. They point out that Earth has gone through many climate changes in its history that are unrelated to human activity. They also argue that the kind of data that is needed to show temperature trends has only been available for the last hundred years or so-too short a time period in which to create a reliable model.

Other scientists argue that even if global warming is occurring, the change in temperature is not enough to warrant such alarm. They point out that many parts of the world experience huge changes in climate regularly with no bad effects. They also argue that gradual temperature changes will be countered by Earth's natural environment, such as the creation of more clouds, and will counteract the warming trends.

38. Which criticism do skeptics have of the data table that shows temperatures increasing?

    F. The data table does not show a clear increase in temperatures.

    G. The data table does not include information from different parts of the world.

    H. The data table does not show a pattern or trend in the data.

    J. The data table does not include temperatures from a long enough period of time.

39. What do scientists who warn of global warming predict about increased evaporation?

    A. They believe that evaporation would cause temperatures to increase even more.

    B. They believe that evaporation would cause temperatures to cool slightly.

    C. They believe that evaporation would cause an increase in the amount of carbon dioxide in the atmosphere.

    D. They believe that evaporation would remove carbon dioxide from the air.

40. Which of the following is NOT an argument used by skeptics about global warming?

    F. Earth's temperature is not increasing any more than other times in history.

    G. Global warming does not cause problems for the environment.

    H. There is no data to indicate that the temperature of Earth is increasing.

    J. Earth's atmosphere responds to global warming to correct it.

STOP